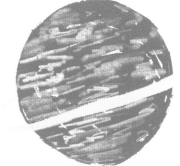

BEE

A story that celebrates our differences

Story and music by
RACHEL FULLER

Illustrations by
EMILIA WHARFE

♭ Play the music ♪

Wherever you see this picture you can listen to the music
from the ballet and create your own movement and dance!
Ask a grown-up to scan the code and click on the track title.

CHAPTER ONE • BEE

Hey! I'm Sprout. Once upon a time
I had a special friend called Bee
who could see and hear things others
couldn't. When Bee looked at flowers
they'd laugh, and the grass would sing
songs. Even the trees seemed more alive,
glowing with beautiful green light when
Bee looked at them.

Bee could also see and talk to fairies like me!
And Bee could fly! – through forests and up
into the sky with us. Sometimes we flew all the
way into space to investigate the planets, stars
and galaxies.

Play the music ♩ ♪

'IN THE PLAYGROUND'

But Bee found school hard. It was tough to pay attention in class and Bee often got in trouble for daydreaming. Even break time was tricky.

One day, Bee came to me feeling sad. "I tried to play with the others, Sprout, but I didn't understand what they were doing."

"You just see and feel things differently from them Bee. It's easy to notice differences like hair colour or height, but it's harder when differences are on the inside. But that's okay. Everyone has things they're good at and things they find tricky. You might not understand the game those kids were playing, but you can see fairies. As for me? I can't swim, but I can fly! Our differences make us special and unique," I explained.

After chatting a bit more, we decided to go for a fly around. But we got so distracted that Bee missed the school bell and ended up being very late for afternoon class.

CHAPTER TWO • AT HOME

When Bee got home, Mum and Dad were arguing.

"Bee needs to be more like the other kids and stop daydreaming, wandering off during breaks and being late for class," Dad said.

"But Bee isn't like the other kids. Bee loves science and the art teacher says Bee is the most talented student she's ever seen!" Mum added.

♭ Play the music ♪

'AT HOME'

Mum and Dad went quiet when Bee walked in.
Bee didn't say anything.

I checked on Bee at bedtime.

"I'm going to try harder," Bee said. "I need to fit
in more. I need to pay attention and not wander
off with you guys. Maybe we can just fly on
weekends?"

CHAPTER THREE • THE SPARKLES

After that, Bee tried really hard to focus at school.

But one day Bee showed up at the fairy circle in the woods behind the school playground while I was in the middle of a band rehearsal. Bee looked upset again.

"It's no good, Sprout," Bee said. "I'm never going to fit in! No matter how hard I try, I can't concentrate for long unless it's something I really enjoy, like art or science. I try to focus but I start thinking about flying or talking to the daffodils and before I know it the class is over and I missed what happened. I've tried playing with the other kids at break, too, but I always mess up and they laugh at me. One of the kids called me 'weird' today and maybe she's right. Maybe I am weird?"

"You're not weird, Bee. Let me show you something . . ."

These are my friends, The Sparkles — the best band in the forest! Gabrielle sings, Kit plays guitar, Zephyr is on drums, Melodia is on keyboards, and Indigo is on bass.

Hey everyone, meet Bee!

Bee, the band is rehearsing a new song called 'Angel'.

Guys, could you play your parts one at a time?"

Kit played the ukulele, making a lovely plinky-plunky sound, like rain on a tin roof, but nicer.

Then Zephyr played his drums and bells, which made Bee start to dance.

I pointed at Melodia next and her fingers moved quickly across the keyboard. The fast, high notes sounded like water in a stream.

Then Indigo played a deep, steady sound on the bass. It was like being underground or in a cave. Bee nodded along in time.

Finally, Gabrielle started to sing, she sounded like an actual angel with her clear, high voice.

♪ Play the music ♪

'ANGEL'

"Don't they sound wonderful?"
I asked Bee.

"They all sound so different,"
Bee said.

"They're all amazing in their
own way, aren't they? It's
not about one of them being
better than the other."

"Absolutely," Bee agreed.

"Now, everyone, play 'Angel' all together."

Zephyr counted them in. They played softly at first, then louder and louder. The music was so magical the flowers started to sing along, the trees clapped their branches and all the animals danced.

Bee laughed with delight and floated up into the air.

"When they all play together it sounds incredible," Bee said, smiling.

Suddenly Bee exclaimed, "Oh my goodness! What time is it? I'm going to be very, very late!"

Bee ran back towards the school playground calling, "See you on Saturday!"

CHAPTER FOUR •
A NEW SCHOOL

When Bee got home, Mum
and Dad were waiting.

"We've found a new school
for you," Dad said.

"We think you'll be happier
there Bee," said Mum.

Bee asked to go and play outside.

We found Bee in the garden with some
tulips, singing a rather sad song.

"Maybe at the new school they can
help me find something I'm really
good at, so I won't get in trouble
for the things I'm not so good at.
Change can be good, right?"

We all agreed. WE could see Bee's magic already.
But fairies see things a bit differently from
humans. The Sparkles told the tulips to cheer up,
and then we all flew around for a bit before Bee's
dinnertime, making sure not to be late.

The next morning, Mum and Dad took Bee to the new school. They met Gertrude, one of the teachers.

"Bee, I'm so glad to meet you. How do you find school?" Gertrude asked Bee.

I whispered to Bee: "I like Gertrude. I think we can trust her. Tell her what you tell me."

Play the music ♪
'BEE AND GERTRUDE'

Bee took a deep breath, then said, "Sometimes everything feels too loud, it hurts my ears, and the light gets too bright. Sometimes I have lots of thoughts all at once, like a traffic jam in my head. It's hard to sit still and stop fidgeting. But I feel calmer in nature and when I fly."

"Fly! That sounds amazing!" exclaimed Gertrude. "Follow me and I'll show you where we make magic here."

She gestured for Bee to follow her.

Bee followed Gertrude down a long corridor into an enormous science laboratory. Bee's eyes lit up.

Behind a long bench stood two children wearing white science coats and safety goggles. They were looking closely at some bright green liquid in a glass flask.

Gertrude introduced the children to Bee. "Meet the twins. Charlotte, Harry, this is Bee."

"Do you like science too?" said the girl.

"Oh yes!" said Bee. "I love inventing things."

"So do we!" said Harry. "Do you want to help us with our experiment?"

Bee asked Gertrude, "Can I?"

"Of course," Gertrude replied. "I'm going to have a quick chat with your parents."

I whispered in Bee's ear, "This place looks amazing. Just be careful not to blow anything up!"

Bee laughed for the first time in ages.

Harry looked over and I'm not completely sure, but I swear he winked at ME!

Play the music

'IN THE LAB'

CHAPTER SIX •
NEW FRIENDS AND ADVENTURES

A couple of days later, I found Bee back
in the lab with Harry and Charlotte.

Harry spotted me right away.

"Hi," he said, looking directly at me.

Bee looked up.

"Um, hi," I replied shyly.

Bee turned to Harry.
"Can you see Sprout?"

"Yes. Charlotte can too."

"Yup! Hi, Sprout!" Charlotte chimed in.

"Next you'll be telling me you can fly as well," said Bee.

Without saying a word, Harry and Charlotte both rose up from the ground and flew over to where I was sitting on the window ledge.

Charlotte asked me, "We usually fly in the woods behind the reservoir. Do you ever fly there?"

"I live in the woods behind Bee's old school, but sometimes my band The Sparkles play in your woods," I explained.

"We LOVE The Sparkles," said Harry.
"I'm learning to play guitar."

"What are you guys working on?" I asked.

"Well," said Bee, "we're working on a new invention together, but something's missing. We've tried everything in the lab."

"Maybe we could fly off for a quick trip into the woods? There's all sorts of magical plants and flowers there," I suggested.

And that's how our adventures began. Over the next few years, Bee, Harry, and Charlotte invented all sorts of amazing things and flew to some amazing places. They always found inspiration in nature. When the teachers asked how they did it, Bee, Harry, and Charlotte would just smile and say, "It's our secret!"

Play the music

'ADVENTURES'

During one of our trips, while the others were off chasing a firefly, Bee, looking serious, suddenly said:

"You know, Sprout, I thought I was weird and different. But I'm not. I've always loved spending time with you and the fairies, but I didn't have anyone on the ground who understood me or who knew how it felt to be different. But there are others like me. I wonder if there are more of us."

Play the music ♪
'I CAN FLY!'

"There are, Bee. More than you might think! Everyone has something they're brilliant at, even if they haven't discovered it yet. Every single person on the planet is special."

EPILOGUE

Bee grew up but kept inventing (and flying with Sprout).

Bee went on to create a new fuel which was kind to the planet and helped the natural world.

You see, we all have our own unique talents and when we share them with others, we make the world a better place!

www.beetheballet.com

RESOURCES

There are lots of wonderful resources to help you or your child identify and make sense of their, or other people's, differences, including:

Autism Misunderstood
autismunderstood.co.uk

The ADHD Foundation
www.adhdfoundation.org.uk

The Curly Hair Project
thegirlwiththecurlyhair.co.uk

You can find more children's books that celebrate our differences at:

Booktrust
www.booktrust.org.uk/booklists/n/books-with-neurodivergent-characters/

Inclusive Books for Children
www.inclusivebooksforchildren.org

ABOUT THE BALLET AND MUSIC FOR BEE

Once upon a time, I wrote a story about a character named BEE. This story was very special because it was based on my own experiences as a child.

I quickly decided that instead of using words, BEE's story should be told through movement and dance. You see, sometimes it's hard, especially when we are young, to say how we feel just with words. But our bodies can show our feelings so clearly through dance and movement.

So, I decided to turn BEE's story into a ballet!

I then composed the music for it. For each part of BEE's adventure, I created music that showed not only how BEE was feeling, but also what was happening in the story.

And that's how BEE's story came to life through beautiful ballet and enchanting music!

A performance of BEE has been co-produced with Royal Ballet and Opera Learning and Participation. You can find out more about it at www.beetheballet.com.

I dedicate this book and music to every child who has ever felt different and struggled to fit in. Also, to all the children around the world who show kindness and compassion when they see another child struggling to find their way.

First published in the UK in 2024 by
Rachel Fuller, in partnership with Whitefox
Publishing

www.wearewhitefox.com

Copyright © Rachel Fuller, 2024

ISBN 9781916797291
Also available as an eBook
ISBN 9781916797307

Illustrations © Rachel Fuller

Edited by Naomi Jones
Designed by Anna Green at Siulen Design
Colour reproduction by BORN London Ltd
Project management by Whitefox Publishing
Printed and bound in Italy by L.E.G.O. SpA